Dea...

Illustrated by Clare Elsom

Raintree

Raintree is an imprint of Capstone Global Library Limited, a company incorporated in England and Wales having its registered office at 7 Pilgrim Street, London, EC4V 6LB – Registered company number: 6695582

www.raintreepublishers.co.uk
myorders@raintreepublishers.co.uk

Text © Capstone Global Library Limited 2013
First published in hardback in 2013
Paperback edition first published in 2014
The moral rights of the proprietor have
been asserted.

Edited by Dan Nunn, Rebecca Rissman, and
  Catherine Veitch
Designed by Philippa Jenkins
Original illustrations © Clare Elsom
Illustrated by Clare Elsom
Production by Victoria Fitzgerald
Originated by Capstone Global Library Ltd
Printed and bound in China

ISBN 978 1 406 25040 4 (hardback)
16 15 14 13 12
10 9 8 7 6 5 4 3 2 1

ISBN 978 1 406 25050 3 (paperback)
17 16 15 14
10 9 8 7 6 5 4 3 2 1

British Library Cataloguing in Publication Data
Thomas, Isabel.
Jealous. -- (Dealing with Feeling...)
152.4'8-dc23
A full catalogue record for this book is available from the British Library.

Contents

Some words are shown in bold, **like this**. Find out what they mean in the glossary on page 23.

What is jealousy?

shy

worried

angry

happy

Jealousy is a **feeling**. It is normal to have many kinds of feelings every day.

Everyone feels jealous sometimes. You might feel jealous if you think someone else is better than you, or if they have something that you want.

How do we know when someone is feeling jealous?

Our faces and bodies can show other people how we are feeling. Also, we may show how we are feeling in the way that we behave.

Some people may become quiet and sad when they feel jealous. Others may behave badly, even towards their friends and family.

What does jealousy feel like?

Jealousy can make you feel sad or grumpy that you do not have what other people have.

You might not feel like being nice to people. Trying to hide jealous **feelings** can make you feel worse.

Is it okay to feel jealous?

If your best friend starts playing with new friends, it can make you feel jealous. You might feel sad or angry, and say nasty things.

It is okay to feel jealous, but it is not okay to be unkind to somebody. You can learn to deal with jealous **feelings,** and be a good friend.

How can I deal with jealousy?

Sometimes jealous **feelings** start because you are worried about something. You might feel worried that your parents do not have enough time to play with you any more.

The best way to deal with feelings is to talk about them. Share your feelings with your parents or friends. They can help you to feel less jealous.

Why should I deal with jealous feelings?

Jealousy can make you feel that you are not as good as other people. It can make you behave **unkindly.**

It is okay to feel jealous, but it is not okay to tease somebody, or to say nasty things about a person. This will make you feel worse.

What should I do when I feel jealous of something?

When somebody has something that you want, it can make you feel jealous. You might want to take what they have to make things seem fair.

It is okay to feel jealous, but it is not okay to take or break someone's **property**. You could deal with jealous **feelings** by doing something that makes you happy.

What should I do when I feel jealous of somebody?

Jealousy can make you feel unhappy when someone else does well. You might feel that you are not good enough.

It is normal to want to do well. Try to be happy when someone else does well, too. Be friendly and say "Well done!"

How can I help someone who is feeling jealous?

Remember that everybody feels jealous sometimes. If you notice someone who is feeling jealous, you can help them to feel better.

When you make new friends, remember
to be kind to your old friends, too.
Share what you have with other people,
and they will share things with you.

Make a jealousy toolbox

Write down some tips to help you deal with jealous **feelings.**

If someone does something well, say "Well done!"

Remember that everyone is different. Our differences make us special.

Think about all the things that make you happy.

Remember that you can always feel proud if you have done your best.

Do something you enjoy.

Try not to compare yourself to other people.

Remember that you will get better if you keep trying at something.

Remember all the things you are good at.

Glossary

feeling something that happens inside our minds. It can affect our bodies and the way we behave.

property something that belongs to someone

unkindly in a nasty way. Being unkind to someone can make them feel sad.

Find out more

Books

All Kinds of Feelings: A Lift-the-Flap Book,
Emma Brownjohn (Tango Books, 2003)

Everyone I See is Luckier than Me: Poems About
Being Jealous, Clare Bevan
(Hodder Children's Books, 2005)

Websites

bbc.co.uk/scotland/education/health/feelings

kidshealth.org/kid/feeling

pbskids.org/arthur/games/aboutface

Index